On
Sketty Sands

Joanna Boulter

ARROWHEAD
PRESS

First published 2001 by:
Arrowhead Press
70 Clifton Road, Darlington,
Co. Durham, DL1 5DX
Tel: (01325) 260741

Typeset and printed by:
Arrowhead Press

Email: arrowhead.press@ntlworld.com

ISBN 0-9540913-0-2

CONTENTS

for the descendants of
William and Eleanor Anne (Nan) Watkins

" … we think back through our mothers if we are women."
Virginia Woolf

ABOVE THE TIDELINE

Fishing float flotsam, green ball that hauled
the drift of a net's full netfall
unsinkably crisscross-cauled,
now cast loose from its catch,
found on my mother's home beach,
and stranded at her hearth
even while we lived where billows
were green grass, shells compressed to chalk.

Witch's ball she called it,
(she, seventh child of a seventh child
who half believed her thoughts could fly
into some nearby mind)
showed me tides in those glassy deeps
as another mother might hold a shell
to her child's ear for the roar and roil –
but she was stone deaf on the starboard side.

Now my mind trawls
in that seagreen swell
with its catch of memories,
each told tale glinting like herring scales,
brig and frigate long ago come to grief
and all hands lost. I'm watching on this coast,
salvaging flotsam, hoping that the tide
hauls up a bottle with a note inside.

IN LOVING MEMORY

My mother's death
has exiled me from that land
that will be deluged
as the tide of *now* rolls in.

I have my passport ready
but the borders have been closed
though I once had free entry,
ran in and out at will.

So while I still see the contours
I trace the map.
Those were my people
their lives my tales:

William and Eleanor Anne,
and their eight children –
Iris, Dolly, Muriel, Stephen,
Eleanor, Marjorie, Nancy, Gwen.

WILLIAM WATKINS, 1868 - 1951

Known to me chiefly by word of mouth,
grandfather who carved tombstones

mild man whose hands
fought death for a third child

and this time won her, rubbing her
with brandy, bringing her back from the brink

to become my mother Nancy. Later she'd wonder
if he was God's Will that they talked about.

She'd tell me how they'd cry
Dadda, sing The Diver!

and he'd take a child on each knee,
and eyes rolling with drama

sing in his basso profundo
of death beneath the waves.

He chose his own tombstone.
Forest of Dean stone, close-grained.

Carved letters say: *beloved husband and father*
bracketed by dates. The terms of a life.

The stone says, Craftsman.

GRANDMA SKETTY IN MAY TIME

Don't you go bringing that stuff indoors now,
not into my house. It means a death.
The children nipped and nibbled the first green shoots
calling them bread-and-cheese. And then each bough
yeasted and creamed, arched foaming overhead.
So pretty, look! No. Like the spittle froth
at the mouth of a dying child. Who could forget?
That heavy scent stank of raw meat, you said.
And cresting sprays tossed like the storm-spun spume
that sucks at sailors. Safe for another year,
once petals dropped and all the paths were scummed.
It's May again, grandmother I never knew.
You're sixty-seven springs dead. Here
are the first words I've addressed to you.

TUNING THE ECHOES

The sisters sang about the house,
solo or in harmony,
discords a temporary squabble
quickly resolved.

Evenings, girls' voices true and clear
above Will's paternal bass, little Nancy's hands
sure on the keyboard. They sound like angels
a neighbour said

and you thought of your golden Marjorie
who could sing seconds to any tune,
now looking down out of heaven's window
still aged three.

Muriel tuned her violin. The sister-angels
joined in, while all the echoes ached
with the missing voice, and the violin case
lay like a baby's coffin.

CHANGELING

The seventh child was dark and undersized,
a scrawny scrap. *Good God* said Will
it's a little goblin. And after the golden gift
of Marjorie, so soon taken. They must have felt
that contrast. The child was always aware of it,
trying to compensate. But still, they meant
to make her their own in naming her.
Will wanted Wilhelmina. *Such an ugly sound*
said Nan, and gave her Nancy.

Her gift was always to see through another's eyes,
to feel another's feelings. And this was her burden
too. She saw imagined disappointments,
unable to believe her company
was wanted for herself.
So many hopeful friendships she let wither
in fear of presuming too much, of standing in a place
meant for another; felt how others felt
only to flinch from breaching privacy.

Sensitive as a sea anemone,
tender in her own skin as a hermit crab,
her logic was nevertheless
intractable as the tide. And like the tide
of dawn-called birdsong surging round the earth
from east to east, she sang her blackbird notes
steadfast as as any bugler,
her cuckoo fears, the echoing rhapsody
of thrushes' song, over and over.

WHO IS REALLY LISTENING?

Now we've all heard the birds singing
the teacher told her class.
Fifty solemn heads nodded. But Nancy
put up her hand and said she'd never
heard them sing. Everyone laughed.
She was sent to stand in the corner
wearing the dunce's cap, still wondering
where anyone had heard robin and thrush
render *Cwm Rhondda* or *Sospan Fach*.
Later, she stomped home bewildered and cross
hearing the sparrows chatter in the gutters,
the blackbirds fluting from the trees.

FRIENDS

Eunice had a face flat as a board.
They'd call after her: *Eunice, Eunice,*
has your mother ironed your face today?
And she'd ignore them, smooth as a folded sheet.

Maggie goggled like a frog. Her eyes bulged.
You mustn't mind me saying so,
said Nancy. *I don't mean to be mean.*
I wouldn't say it if it wasn't true.
Maggie, pop-eyed, said she quite understood.

Another girl wore her school pinny
the right way for three days, then inside out
Thursdays and Fridays. Nancy thought
this was so clever, couldn't see
why Mamma wouldn't let her do it too
– think of the laundry it would save.

Then there was the small boy
asked by a neighbour what his cat was called.
Go on, urged his Mam, *say Fluff, mun.*
And dull as doodahdi the child said *Fuffmun.*

A foreign boy was staying down the road.
We have soon Eastern. I wish you a merry and a happy ones.
They helped him with his English, taught him to swear,
told him *shwglych y bwglych* was Welsh for *shake the bottle.*
He believed them. They called him a dull bugger.
Me dull bugger, he said, pleased.

THE TALE MY UNCLE TOLD ME

See that barn, there? There's a story to that.
You had a ancestor was a buccaneer;
and he went pirating off to the Caribbean,
come home again with a shipload of gold.
Well, maybe not so much, shared with the crew –
but a nice little fortune for one.
So, soon's they get within sight of the Worm's Head,
your ancestor (who was a clever man, see,
like all his descendants), he calls up the crew,
proposes a swearing match. Winner gets the lot.
Well now, they're all for it. Not a man there
but prided himself on his tongue for oaths.
So they set turns, began to fire away.
And the curses thundered out like cannonballs
spat from between their teeth, could have blown holes
in a Portugoose or a Spanish man o' war.
Imagine that lot, yelling the French to rout!
But no man a clear best. Well, your ancestor,
he waited them all out. Sense of drama, see.
Till they were shoving him, saying Go on mun.
Then he stepped forward, planted his feet firm
on the heaving deck, threw back his mighty head
– *duw, duw*, he was a fine man, mun –
and he opened his mouth and began.

13

Well damn your eyes mun, he said; but that
was only the start. Oaths flowed from him
like wine from a cask. He was uncorked all right.
The style of him! Never a misplaced damn,
never a bloody adrift. *Ach y fi*
was nothing to him. Flaming buggers of hell
he called them, blisters on the bum of God,
the Devil's emeroids; said they hadn't the wit
to piss downwind (I'm only quoting, mind);
told them to frig their bloody ear'oles clean
and listen to him; told them to get their brains
out of their britches, give 'em room to think.
And there was more: Hell got more colourful
under his bruising tongue; the griddled bones
of saints were flaming, fit to scorch your ears.
His rhetoric whanged the air with cutlass words.
And all the time
the rhythm of it running like the swell
of his own element. The *huyl* was on him.

And then a moment's calm, like the dog days,
before a storm of shouting, whistling, cheering –
because the others weren't a patch on him.
They were a load of miserable buggers,
couldn't string enough oaths from the yardarm
to hang a cat. So, guess who won? No contest!
And there's the barn he built with his pirate gold.
But *duw*, he was a fine man, mun.

THE ONION, MEMORY

Onions chopped into *cawl* become the broth.
But peeling the onion leaves nothing to find
till the roasted centre layer by layer unspools
slithering slim and hot to comfort earache.

For all that, Nancy's eardrum burst –
so that ever after she'd cock her head
birdlike toward sounds, watch lips for words.

Stories around the fire: each *do you remember?*
or *what about ...?* slips off another layer,
leaving me only a slippery transient shape,
nothing to hold, a proxy memory.

SHIP'S LOGBOOK

Echoes of soundings; lists of stores;
names of ratings, live out of history.
Almost as soon as she'd learned to read
Nancy would pore over the heirloom book,
its copperplate written by gimballed lantern
in the dark watches, imagine herself there
on Lieutenant Richards' ship, in the Admiral's fleet.

The step on the stairs, that always-squeaky floorboard,
were the creak of ship's timbers, the knock
of spars. All night she lay at anchor
hove-to with Gwenny in the sagging double bed.
A hammock. It swayed gently with the soft
swell of their breath. Oak Cottage, ship of the line.

Branches shook in the breeze, the rigging swayed.
She thought of the tars atop in crow's-nest and ratlines;
the straining sails, the proud array of flags.
But the powder-monkeys
were her age, darting between juddering guns,
avoiding the recoil, mad with the clamour closed
between low decks, the battle's heat and stink.
And then the tattered cheer from smoke-tight throats
that stung with salt to hear how Nelson fell.

In the shipwreck of Dadda's death, the logbook foundered,
went down with all hands when Oak Cottage was cleared.

NOT LIKE US

Mary Richards, gentleman's daughter,
waltzed through the round of balls and calls,
played to perfection a young belle's part.
An unsuitable suitor caught her eye.
Her family whisked her safe away –
and her host's young coachman won her heart.
So the two of them fled to a life together –
harbour to harbour, bay to bay.

Somethin' a bit – you know – there
's what I 'eard. Good fam'ly, mind.
Now she's doin' her own work –
'ear 'er bread, smellin' all down the road?

No one knows how they made their journey.
He knew the highway's twists and turns,
but he was known at each coaching inn
for thirty miles as the black crows fly.
Perhaps they sailed with the white-maned horses
from Milford Haven to Swansea Bay,
while the drowned lay deep in deceitful waters
harbour to harbour, bay to bay.

An' all those babies – anyone know 'ow long – ?
Well at least 'e married 'er.
D'you think they had to pay 'im?

The iron horse coughed smoke and soot,
sullied her muslin, jolted bones.
Fear of discovery braced her taut
though her trusting hand in Stephen's lay,
as she wept for her parents, smiled to think
of that bright new life she'd build with him.
And the train forged on its rhythmic way
harbour to harbour, bay to bay.

Managin' all right for a posh lady
come from over by 'Averfordwest.
Well they're all English over by there
aren't they? Not like us.

Not like us. Always for her the bit
of family money, her children with soles to their boots
and the chance of schooling. Always,
for her, the memory of the former life,
the correct speech, the manners and music
in that little cottage in Vivian Road.
The poetry book of 1869
(the year before you, grandmother, were born
her seventh child), that book that I now have.

OSTRICH FEATHERS

William James, come sailing home at last
with gifts for his sisters,
and for another.

Those feathers in the gloom of the bazaar
had gleamed white as her skin.
One for Nan and one for Lizzie, stowed
in his sea-chest; but that other,
the one for Millie, his declaration
he could not hide away.

He stroked the plumes, imagined the soft gold
of her hair beneath his touch, he saw and sighed
as that sensuous curve and droop kissed at her cheek.
Running his finger down the slender quill
he thought her spine, glimpsed at the nape, must be
delicate like that, and as fine.
The filaments trembled with his breath.

Two more voyages for his Master's Ticket —
a trophy to offer a bride.
He knew his sisters thought her a featherhead.
But all the way home those long sea-leagues he nerved
himself to speak, to say *I love her, Nan*

so that the dignity of his love
gleamed like his honest heart:
won her, and them.

TRIPTYCH

Mamma sits at the back door
for the coolth.

She whips cream on a blue plate.

The knife cuts and cuts,
lifts and lifts.

It will be ready
when she can tip the plate right up
without those white clouds moving.

                    *

When an aeroplane buzzes overhead
Nancy and Gwenny want to be nearer,

clamber on the roof of the *tŷ bach*
annoying the occupant

jumping and waving like mad,
and tumbling off
amid gales of giggles.

                    *

The screech of iron on stone
slices the air.
A cart slithers down Sketty Hill
the drag heaved out behind –
a brake, a land-anchor
to keep the tide of gravity
from swamping cart and horse.

YOUR DROWNED BROTHER

You were thirteen when the Mumbles lifeboat
was swamped and foundered, just too far from shore.
And the women of Mumbles Head
knotted their shawls into ropes and fished for their men,
screaming like gulls above the storm, then braced
grimly silent to pull. One man was saved.

One man: for all those women baptised by the sea
into such a sisterhood, then and forever!
Whose was he? Never mind. He was all of theirs:
and yet no more than they were each others' now,
conjoined by the knotted shawls, the gripped hands.

So the tale of his saving swelled throughout the Gower,
roared in the echoing ear as the wind died down –
so that the other women, thinking O
if it had been my Dai,
gathered in knots in the dying storm,
and clutching their shawls around them knew themselves
cousins to such a feat.

You were not quite a woman,
your thoughts tide-turning between
father and *lover* or *husband.* It was *brother* perhaps,
that soon-to-be-sailor, held
your fears. And who knows what he thought?

He was too far out in the Bristol Channel
when the cargo shifted; too far
for your arms to reach and haul him in
as the Mumbles women did for that lifeboatman
when you were both children; too far out
to shawl him in in the Welsh fashion,
swaddle his body like one of your dead infants.

But still you watch each storm,
squinting through salt-stiff squalls
for the drowned face and floating hair,
for the white arm in the foam.

Lost at sea. No corpse ever came home.
There was no gravestone where
that other William could chisel
lapidary words, no place to go and grieve.
What you are doing is reading his epitaph
in the impermanence of water, with the wind's
voice, which is his breath, and yours.

SNAPSHOT ON SKETTY SANDS, 1923

On a calm day, the box-brownie lines up
the arm of the bay, looking out toward
Mumbles Head and beyond. It's low tide.

No angry water. Ripples plash warm
on naked feet. No killing cold,
no undertow, snatching. The swell breathes gently.

Three children on Sketty Sands. Nancy has on
her school gymslip and straw hat, Gwenny
a summer frock. They're barefoot in a pool

of shallow water held by a wall of sand
that echoes the headland's shape. Above their heads
their arching outer arms reflect this curve.

Between them they're holding by the hands
a sturdy three-year-old, Iris's daughter,
a second Marjorie. The camera frames them

amateurishly off-centre; but she's
the unselfconscious pivot of the pattern,
enfolded by those three embracing arcs.

Encompassed, familiar:
this is how the sea is made safe.

"LITTLE NANCY AND GWENNY, SUCH CLEVER CHILDREN"

Thrown into pair closeness
by the inconsolable deaths of sisters,
playing neighbours called themselves
Mrs Jones and Mrs Davis.

Minding their beanstick house they would exclaim
Gawdle-mighty look at the time –
not a child washed nor a po emptied!
This won't buy the baby a new bonnet!

As they grew older
they called their budding tits Florrie and Ethel,
their first tides rising
a game to them still.

Iris, already married,
warned them what to expect.
As Mamma hadn't with her,
not knowing how to speak

of such indelicacy, thinking perhaps
tomorrow's time enough, she's still a child.
Until there was suddenly no more time –
and the girl thought she was dying.

But she saw her sisters safely confident.
Few fears for them. Curious enough
to answer secretly an advertisement –
a sample under a plain wrapper.

And Mamma's sister, the unembarrassed spinster,
said *you could stuff it with soft paper,*
so that they shrieked *Auntie Lizzie!*
whatever for? giggling all along the beach.

BURLINGTON BERTIE OF BOW

The parlour's a concert room in miniature.
How to loosen her hips for the elegant slouch
and saunter? – when the hearthrug stage constrains
her step, and a flicked coat-tail would send
half an audience of photos tumbling.

Dolly tucks an imaginary cane
under her arm, puts up her silky chin –
have I got the shoulders right, Nance?
The invisible gloves slick to her hands like skin.
Her soprano flirts with a row of bearded uncles.

On the night, aspidistras and faded velvet
frame the stage, and on rows of wooden chairs
Nancy sits with the others, good ear cocked,
critical of the pianist, laughing at the jokes,
fidgetty with nerves for her sister.

Now there's room for the seven strides to the turn
at the end of the phrase, buttoning grey kid gloves.
She's nonchalant in a hired morning coat.
Chestnut hair tucked under the topper,
she eyes up the audience, preens in song.

GRANDMA SKETTY'S YEAR

Year by year rocking the babies
chanting the months to soothe their cries

> *Januairy*
> *Februairy*
> *Mars*
> *Avreel*

Bouncing the children, making them giggle
at the known year in its daft disguise

> *Mye*
> *June*
> *Jupiter*
> *Jalott*

Watching them grow as the years press on you,
pulling white hairs and stifling sighs

> *Ocopontober and November*
> *and fifty more if you care to mention 'em*

However you name it, time still flies.

HOSPITAL SHIP

That must have been the worst week ever –
worse than the little deaths with their huge agonies
(tiny Eleanor, Marjorie's promise quenched),
than Willie's drowning with its seas of grief –

that fearful week and more when Muriel lay
brain-fevered, Gwenny with pneumonia,
both of them out of their heads and at death's door.

Oak Cottage was rigged up like a hospital ship.
An invalid to each of the double beds
in the girls' room. Dolly sharing the nursing
with you, sisters-in-law, neighbours helping out.
Iris of course in Shropshire with her babies.
Stephen packed off to Aunty Mary's.
His truckle bed, in that tiny slip of a room,
for any nurse that could be spared a while,
what sleep was possible, in such a nightmare.

Only the one tap, and that outside –
Aunty Mary took those fevered sheets
away to boil. Neighbours brought food. As you
had done, would do, when they'd their troubles.

And Nancy. Nancy on the couch downstairs
scarcely able to move for swollen joints,
yet not in danger of death,
needing not so much nursing

as comfort, a bit of *maldod* for her pain.
And you, distracted, pausing when you could
to kiss and smooth her hair and tuck her in,
neglecting her, knowing she understood.

But you put all your strength into the battle,
had no reserves to call on when your own
skirmish began, that wore you down so soon.
Gwenny recovered. Nancy's pain, suppressed,
welled up throughout her life. Poor Muriel,
that lovely girl, was stranded fierce and thin
upon a hostile beach, never the same again.

The hospital ship drifted those next few years
inexorably pulled towards the shoals.
Mu lasted longer; but you'd fought too hard
for those you loved. Dwindled away.
And left them pilotless.

A MOUSE'S NEST FOR GRANDMA SKETTY

You would lie propped while Nancy brushed your hair
gently, slowly. They all knew you were failing,
tried to believe it wasn't true. Hard cold
softened towards spring for your last season,
buds coloured, began to fuzz the hedgerows;
and after college Nancy brushed your hair
not speaking of its faded lifelessness,
the way it fell. You were deciduous,
your winter out of time. Hair lay like leaves
on pillow and coverlet, choked the brush each day.
Nancy gathered it, head held down to hide
the raindrops' fall, wound it around her finger.
You laid a bird-boned hand
on hers and murmured *Look, a mouse's nest*
to keep the baby mice all nice and warm.

GOING DOWN HOME

You going down home this year?
Me neither. Seems an age.
The wires dipped and rose
(Shropshire to Surrey to Salisbury Plain)
with the singsong voices as the sisters spun
Sketty out of the air: those humming strings,
binding the four of them, the tune of home
that echoed in their voices day to day.

Daffodils brought it on;
or, turning the radio dial, catching a snatch
of a male voice choir down from up the valleys
singing *Myfanwy* with a tone like shammy-leather.
And hearing with nostalgia's ear
the sounds of Newport or the Rhondda,
Cardiff or Swansea, in a stranger's voice,
they'd always speak, the lilt of recognition
rhyming involuntarily on the tongue.

I got the shadow of a language
in my mother's speech: but hers
was englished onto the matrix
of unspoken Welsh.
As the starling tunes to the blackbird, hearing perhaps
a something beyond its reach.
And *Calon Lân*, or a Swansea voice in the street,
tugs at my resonances too, vibrating strings
that amplify these hand-me-down harmonics.

*

It's not *down home* for me, although I feel
the pull and twang. A singsong echo's not
language enough to claim a nation by.
The sisters' voices lilting down the wires
built home each time for them, and let us in.
But now our passports are revoked, for they
are all gone home for good.